Bram Stoker's *DRACULA:*

A Centennial Exhibition
at the Rosenbach Museum & Library
April 10–November 2, 1997

Wendy Van Wyck Good
Curator

Michael J. Barsanti
Assistant Curator

*With an Introduction
by* Nina Auerbach

Philadelphia 1997

FRONT JACKET ILLUSTRATION:
Copyright Maurice Sendak, 1997.

BACK JACKET:
First edition of Bram Stoker's *Dracula*
(London: Archibald Constable and Company, 1897).
Photograph by Joan Broderick.

FRONT FLAP
Vlad Tepes, in a hand-colored 15th-century woodcut

BACK FLAP
A calendar page on which Stoker plotted the action of *Dracula*

Library of Congress Catalog Card Number: 97-66392
ISBN 0-939084-29-5

© 1997 Rosenbach Museum & Library

PRINTED IN THE UNITED STATES OF AMERICA

Foreword. Not all the treasures of the Rosenbach Museum & Library were acquired by the museum's founders, Philip and Dr. A.S.W. Rosenbach. Bram Stoker's manuscript notes and outlines for *Dracula* came to the collections by purchase in 1970, nearly twenty years after the Rosenbach opened its doors. The *Dracula* notes are, however, the kind of acquisition that would have delighted the Rosenbach brothers.

Philip Rosenbach (1863–1953) and Dr. A.S.W. Rosenbach (1876–1952) established the Rosenbach Company in 1903. During their half-century in business together, they proved themselves not only as dealers in fine and decorative arts (Philip's domain) and in rare books and manuscripts (the Doctor's) but also as personal collectors. Philip formed the core of our art collections; the Doctor, our rare book and manuscript holdings. While the art collections reflect a mixed level of connoisseurship, occasionally rising to the very highest standards, the books and manuscripts reflect the Doctor's stringent standards for personal collecting. He once quipped that if there were more than five known copies of an item, he wouldn't have it at home. His collections comprise only the rarest of the rare, selected according to three criteria: condition, significance, and rarity. Bram Stoker's manuscript notes for *Dracula* meet all three of those criteria—in spades.

This centennial celebration of *Dracula* would have greatly pleased the Rosenbach brothers, fulfilling—as it does in part—their stated mission for this museum: fostering knowledge of art, literature, and history. We hope that in this celebration of Bram Stoker's greatest achievement, the serious student of literature and the vampire devotee (or neophyte) alike will learn something new. That is what the Rosenbach brothers would have wanted, and it is what we hope we have achieved.

Wendy Van Wyck Good, curator of exhibitions, planned the exhibition and wrote the catalog text. When, four months before the exhibition opening, Wendy left the Rosenbach to care for her twins, then in utero, Michael Barsanti, a graduate student at the University of Pennsylvania, completed the project. Michael had come to the Rosenbach as an intern under a grant from the Fels Fund to work on our celebrated exhibition *Making It New: Marianne Moore and the Visual Arts* (November 1996–March 1997). We are grateful that Michael could extend his good work with us to include *Dracula*.

The Rosenbach appreciates the generosity that has made this centennial celebration possible. The Rosenbach's exhibition program is supported by the museum's membership and trustees and by grants from the National Endowment for the Humanities; the Institute of Museum Services; the Pennsylvania Historical and Museum Commission; the Pennsylvania Council on the Arts; and the Philadelphia Cultural Fund. We thank the trustees of the Phoebe W. Haas Charitable Trust for their support of our educational programs, including this exhibition and catalog. The Young Friends of the Rosenbach sponsored a *Save Dracula!* benefit to fund conservation of the manuscript notes; the success of their effort will indeed allow Dracula to live into the 21st century, as their gala's slogan promised. W. W. Norton & Company became a corporate member of the Rosenbach with a generous contribution of 200 copies of its new critical edition of *Dracula*. Maurice Sendak, bibliophile of the first rank, has continued his long-time support of the Rosenbach by contributing the original illustration for the catalog cover. We thank Professor Nina Auerbach of the University of Pennsylvania for sharing with us her unparalleled understanding of *Dracula* and for preparing the catalog introduction. Susan Schindler contributed her services as catalog copy editor. With this catalog, Greer Allen has demonstrated again his superb talent as a designer.

We also thank the individuals and institutions that have loaned items for this exhibition and the staff members who assisted us: Dr. Joseph Bierman, Baltimore; The Athenaeum of Philadelphia and Dr. Roger W. Moss; The Book Sail, Orange County, California, and John McLaughlin; Bram Stoker Memorial Association, New York, and Jeanne Youngson; Fales Library, New York University, New York, and Marvin Taylor; The Free Library of Philadelphia, Theatre Collection, and Geraldine Duclow; Harry Ransom Humanities Research Center, the University of Texas at Austin, and Debra Armstrong-Morgan; and the University of Pennsylvania, Van Pelt Library, Special Collections, and Lynne Farrington.

Finally, without a special and especially generous gift from Dr. Andrea M. Baldeck and William M. Hollis, Jr., this catalog could not have been sent to press. We are grateful for their continuing support of the Rosenbach, which in this instance has given enthusiasts and scholars a permanent record of the Rosenbach's centennial celebration of Bram Stoker's *Dracula*.

STEPHEN K. URICE
Director
February 1997

Introduction. Dracula has proved himself a vampire for all seasons. This year, he turns one hundred—a fraction of his great age but an impressive birthday to most mortals. His contemporaries would scarcely have expected his centenary to be celebrated in America from coast to coast or commemorated at venerable institutions such as Philadelphia's Rosenbach Museum and Library: in 1897, Bram Stoker's *Dracula* was one of many fantastic adventure stories—and, according to reviewers, a relatively pedestrian one—in which manly Englishmen fought foreign monsters. Stoker's King Vampire has outlived Robert Louis Stevenson's Mr. Hyde, Rider Haggard's Ayesha, H. G. Wells' Martians, and George du Maurier's Svengali, largely because he is so suavely adaptable.

Unlike his monstrous contemporaries and unlike the vampires who preceded him in British horror literature, Dracula is a shapeshifter. Not only can he turn into wolf, bat, rat, or mist at need, but the stately, white-whiskered, if lupine old gentleman we meet in Transylvania also becomes a vigorous young lecher when he gets to London's Piccadilly Circus. By the time our heroes expel him, he is sporting a chic straw hat.

Bram Stoker claims that Dracula was destroyed, but throughout the twentieth century he has continued to mutate, especially in American movies. As decades pass, he grows younger, sexier, and more sensitive, just as he would have chosen. In 1931, Bela Lugosi turned him into a Valentino-like seducer, giving him a foreign accent and an opera cape that would have embarrassed Stoker's trendy invader of modernity. In 1979, Frank Langella made him the idol of a feminist decade: a mercurial liberator sympathetic to oppressed women, apologetic even at having to bite them. Gary Oldman turned him into an exotic mourner in 1992: this lugubrious *fin-de-siècle* Dracula is so busy weeping over his dead wife that he has lost even his hunger.

Dracula's latest incarnation is an appropriate elegy for a country mourning its lost great days, but if in twentieth-century America, Dracula has become increasingly domesticated, he is currently one of the few role models the young embrace. A supposedly floundering generation dresses as Goths in black clothes and make-up and plays an intricate role-playing game called *The Masquerade,* whose characters are named after Stoker's. At one hundred, Dracula has lost some of his bloodlust, but unlike most monsters and mortals of his generation, he is aggressively young.

America's compliant companion is far from Stoker's original character. In 1897, Dracula was truly nasty. He smelled; he was less lithe than bloated with blood; he gloated over his power rather than tenderly eliciting the powers of mortals. Critics impale him as the epitome of all sorts of unlikable Victorian traits: imperialism, xenophobia, homophobia, capitalism, and masturbation are only some of his uncongenial attributes. In his time, Dracula was not convivial. Compared to earlier vampires, he is so lacking in tact that he was unlikely to have appealed even to his author, who, as manager of Henry Irving's renowned Lyceum Theatre, was adept at smoothing over troubled situations.

Most critics assume that Dracula was a shadow portrait of Henry Irving, the great actor who was Stoker's revered employer, or at least a character Stoker hoped Irving might play in a theatrical adaptation. Irving would have been appalled to be remembered today as the inspiration for his underling's repellent creation, but Bram Stoker's creature is not really Irving; he is a distillation of Irving's single-mindedness, his will to conquer, his alienation from ordinary life. Unlike the vampire, Irving could be convivial, even cheeky, but the England Dracula invades does resemble Irving's gorgeous empire, the Lyceum Theatre.

The ornate Lyceum exuded conspicuous consumption and cultural uplift. Like England itself, Irving's Lyceum was grand, solid, and implacably patriarchal. Because of Irving's achievement, the disreputable stage found itself for the first time in the vanguard of Victorian art and culture. Yet Stoker saw the price of this cultural primacy. Irving was always overspending, never saving: his theater's appearance of solidity was built on sand. Only outsiders were surprised when in 1898, he had to relinquish his control over the Lyceum to a syndicate.

The Lyceum family had always been a brilliant fiction. Onstage, Irving paternally engulfed his radiant partner, the beloved actress Ellen Terry. But while the Lyceum made Ellen Terry famous, it thwarted her as an artist. Irving was too solemn and stately to stage the comedies she loved; he refused, in fact, to stage any play that did not highlight his own magnificence. Throughout the 1890s, Ellen Terry aged into increasing agitation and barely suppressed rage at her diminishing roles in rickety vehicles for Irving. Stoker wrote much chivalrous gush about Ellen Terry, but he observed her as well. Like Ellen Terry, the women in *Dracula* are uneasy in their roles even before the vampire comes. Like her in her rages, they show sinister and unexpected powers once bitten. During Stoker's long career at the Lyceum, he saw the fissures in imperial British society and the hierarchical English family. His life in a powerful theatrical company imperceptibly coming apart gave him the material to articulate fears that reached beyond the stage.

Like the Lyceum and the England it mirrored, the civilization Dracula attacks is, on the surface, bursting with prosperity and power, but even before the vampire comes, it is consuming itself with fear of its own dying. It may be this unspoken awareness of an impaled community that makes Dracula so important to modern America. He feasts less on blood than on social and spiritual bankruptcy. He comes to warn us that we don't believe in what we pledge or who we say we are. The living death he carries is a mirror of society's own.

Dracula has been an indelible part of American life; it is fitting that Philadelphia, where America first defined itself, houses the notes where Bram Stoker first imagined him. I have never felt Dracula's presence more intimately than when I read Stoker's notes in the Rosenbach Library, at the cultural heart of Philadelphia. I was working, on a tight deadline, on my book *Our Vampires, Ourselves* and had reserved a place at the Rosenbach some weeks before—on what turned out to be the eeriest and most dangerous day of the terrible winter of 1994. Philadelphia had been petrified by an ice storm; the city was frozen in deadly glitter. The Rosenbach, like everything else, was closed, but its wonderful staff had preternaturally managed to get there. I was told that the Stoker notes were waiting for me if I could make it in.

The three-block journey, dragging my laptop computer over frozen streets, felt as thrillingly dangerous as Jonathan Harker's excursion through waste and night to the vertigo of Dracula's castle. At the Rosenbach, the staff was as cheerfully welcoming as Dracula was to Jonathan, though far less menacing. Sitting alone with Bram Stoker in Mr. Rosenbach's empty mansion while the ice drummed on his elegant windows, I have never felt so close to vampires. Bram Stoker has particularly insane and inscrutable handwriting; only his master Henry Irving surpasses him in fiendish illegibility. Ordinarily, going through his manuscripts would have been something of a chore, but the simultaneous courtesy and creepiness of the Rosenbach was, on that scary day, an inspiration. Bram Stoker's vision sprang back to life, or to undeath, through the setting in which I read his papers.

The Rosenbach isn't always as menaced or its staff as valiant as they were on that frozen day in 1994, but infallibly, they restore dead visions to life—even when those visions are as chilling as Bram Stoker's were. The present exhibition reminds us that the living dead are not always harbingers of doom and hidden blight. Sometimes, like those at the Rosenbach, vampires bring with them gifts from the forgotten past.

NINA AUERBACH

The Provenance of Bram Stoker's notes for *Dracula*. When the existence of the *Dracula* notes at the Rosenbach first became known to literary scholars in the mid-1970s, the natural question was: How did they get here? Since then, like Harker and company pursuing the Count, we have been on the trail of their provenance, which has moved in and out among the shadows and the light of public knowledge. Having knitted together in chronological order every scrap of evidence as Mina did, we are not, at the time of writing, able to show a whole connected narrative, but the hunt is still on in several quarters. We will announce any further findings, and welcome all additional information and suggestions.

When the question arose we began our search, of course, with the Philadelphia firm of Charles Sessler, from whom we bought the notes in 1970, but extensive research in the firm's records at the Historical Society of Pennsylvania failed to find the source of the notes.

It had always been known that the notes were sold with other books and manuscripts from Stoker's library by Sotheby, Wilkinson & Hodge on 7 July 1913 — the last time they appeared in the auction record. For some time nobody seemed to know who bought them, but recently two annotated copies of the catalog have come to light, both identifying the purchaser of lot 182 as "Drake." This was the New York bookseller James F. Drake, who sold several other items he purchased at this sale to the Rosenbach Company the following month. Unfortunately, he does not seem to have offered *Dracula*. Research to date in his firm's records at the Harry Ransom Humanities Research Center at the University of Texas at Austin indicates that if any record of the notes remains, it must be in the correspondence files, and so far the most likely names have yielded nothing.

Twenty-five years after Drake bought them, the notes reappeared in the possession of Charles Scribner's Sons, which offered them for sale in no less than four catalogs between 1938 and 1946. Unfortunately, the Scribner Archive at the Grolier Club does not have the sales records for the crucial period, nor any other indication of the notes' source or purchaser. The trail disappears again until 1970, when the Rosenbach bought the notes from Sessler.

Our thanks to Donald C. Dickinson; Eric Holzenberg and the late Allen Asaf of the Grolier Club; Bill Fagelson of the Harry Ransom Humanities Research Center; Lynn Hensen; Linda Stanley of the Historical Society of Pennsylvania; Saundra Taylor of the Lilly Library, Indiana University; Ronald R. Randall; Charles Scribner III; and all the others who have helped in the search.

ELIZABETH E. FULLER
Librarian
February 1997

Bram Stoker

1 Beginnings.

Abraham Stoker was born in 1847 in Clontarf, a seaside town just north of Dublin. Struck by a mysterious ailment, he spent his early childhood as an invalid, unable to walk until he was seven. During his years of bed rest, Abraham was tenderly cared for by his father, a civil servant at Dublin Castle, and his mother, Charlotte, a native of Sligo, Ireland. Both parents sat by his bed telling him stories, his father discussing history and the theater, his mother recounting Irish folk tales. Charlotte vividly recalled the years of famine during her youth, when some were forced to drink the blood of the family cow. Abraham especially enjoyed her stories of the terrible 1832 cholera epidemic, in which those afflicted with the disease were sometimes, in haste, buried alive.

Abraham, who later shortened his name to Bram, regained his health by the time he was a young man. When he entered Trinity College in Dublin in 1863, he was an impressive figure standing over six feet tall, who excelled in athletics as well as academics. He was active in student life and participated in two of the most prestigious university clubs, The Philosophical Society and The Historical Society, Trinity's debating group. In 1866, Bram followed his father to Dublin Castle, where he became Clerk to the Registrar of Petty Sessions. Although he found the work uninspiring, Stoker performed his duties admirably and was promoted to Inspector of Petty Sessions. In 1879, he published his first book, *The Duties of Clerks of Petty Sessions in Ireland*, a carefully researched reference work designed to assist clerks with their duties in the complex Irish court system. Although occupied during the day at Dublin Castle, Stoker spent his evenings in the Dublin theaters. In 1871, he contacted the editors of the Dublin *Evening Mail* and volunteered his services as a drama critic, a post he held for five years. Before long, the shadowy, fantastic world of the theater became more real and vital to Stoker than his office job at Dublin Castle.

Although little is known of their early courtship, Stoker became engaged to nineteen-year-old Dubliner Florence Balcombe (1858–1935) in 1878. Stoker was Florence's second suitor; the first was Oscar Wilde. After meeting her in 1876, Wilde became infatuated with the beautiful Florence, sending her romantic letters and even sketching her portrait. Wilde was surprised, and undoubtedly hurt, to learn of her engagement to Stoker. Stoker married Florence in December 1878, just as he resigned from Dublin Castle to accept a full-time position as acting manager of the Lyceum Theatre in London.

Stoker published several short stories as a young man, but his first major literary achievement came at age thirty-five with the 1882 publication of *Under the Sunset*, a collection of fairy tales inspired by his mother's stories of the cholera epidemic. The book, dedicated to Stoker's son and only child, Noel, born in 1879, is preoccupied with the forces of good and evil, examines the boundaries between life and death, and makes use of Gothic themes and imagery. Many critics have drawn parallels between Stoker's fairy tales and his crowning achievement, *Dracula*, which appeared fifteen years later. Clearly, the seeds for Stoker's vampire novel were sown in his earlier works of Gothic fiction.

> *"In my babyhood I used, I understand, to be often at the point of death. Certainly till I was about seven years old I never knew what it was to stand upright."*
>
> BRAM STOKER

PHOTOGRAPH OF BRAM STOKER.
From *Henry Irving* by Laurence Irving
(London: Faber and Faber, 1951).
Reproduced with the permission of John H.B. Irving

OSCAR WILDE (1854–1900). PORTRAIT OF FLORENCE BALCOMBE, AUGUST 1876.
Pencil on paper, 15 x 12½ inches
On loan from the Art Collection, Harry Ransom Humanities Research Center, The University of Texas at Austin

FLORENCE STOKER'S OPERA GLASSES.
On loan from the Bram Stoker Memorial Association, New York

UNDER THE SUNSET
(London: Sampson Low, 1882).
On loan from the Bram Stoker Memorial Association, New York

Shown here is an illustration of the "invisible giant," a personification of the plague, as it descends across the city. Notice the boy who stares from his window at the approaching pestilence, much as Stoker must have observed the world from his window as an invalid child.

II Henry Irving.

Bram Stoker first saw Henry Irving (1838–1905) on 28 August 1867 at the Royal, a Dublin theater. Irving, who was playing the role of Captain Absolute in *The Rivals*, electrified the audience with his powerful, instinctive performance. At the time, the twenty-nine-year-old actor was embarking on a brilliant career in the theater. Within a few years, he would become the most popular star in Britain, as heroic a figure in the nineteenth century as Laurence Olivier would be in the twentieth. Years later, in December 1876, Stoker attended a Dublin performance of *Hamlet* with Irving in the title role and wrote a glowing review of the actor's controversial interpretation of the play. Irving, undoubtedly flattered, invited the young drama critic to join him for dinner at his rooms in the Shelbourne Hotel. The two talked until dawn and met again the following evening, when Irving recited Thomas Hood's poem "The Dream of Eugene Aram." At the end of the recitation, the actor collapsed with emotion. Stoker was so moved by the performance that he was struck with "something like a violent fit of hysterics." From that point forward, Stoker was forever devoted to Irving.

In November 1878, Irving secured the lease on the Lyceum Theatre in London and decided to form his own acting company. He asked Stoker to leave Dublin and move to London to become "acting manager" of the theater. Stoker eagerly accepted the invitation. As acting manager, he was responsible for handling correspondence (Stoker once estimated that he had written nearly half a million letters on Irving's behalf), supervising a staff of one hundred and twenty-eight, and making arrangements for theatrical tours, both in England and abroad. (Between 1883 and 1904, the Lyceum Theatre toured the United States eight times; Stoker organized all of these trips.) On a typical day at the theater, Stoker would leave home late in the morning, work through the afternoon and evening, and return home at sunrise. This was not, perhaps, the most agreeable situation for his new wife, Florence, but she was able to divert herself with a busy social schedule.

"We understood each other's nature, needs and ambitions, and had a mutual confidence, each towards the other in his own way, rare amongst men."
BRAM STOKER

A letter from Bram Stoker as acting manager of the Lyceum Theatre, 1891

Stoker served as acting manager of the Lyceum Theatre for twenty-eight years. Despite Stoker's almost obsessive devotion, Irving remained aloof and rarely recognized his acting manager's talents and abilities. Irving's domineering personality had a considerable impact on Stoker's life and work. In fact, many critics suggest that Irving, who was known for his chilling portrayals of villains from Mephistopheles to Macbeth, was the primary model for the character of Count Dracula. As Stoker began compiling notes for *Dracula* in the early 1890s, he clearly envisioned the yet unwritten novel as a stage production, with Irving in the title role. Stoker realized that the character of Count Dracula, perhaps one of the most unforgettable villains in literary history, was also the perfect vehicle for Irving.

After Irving's death, Stoker began writing *Personal Reminiscences of Henry Irving*, a flattering and subjective account of the actor's life. Stoker was able to undertake this task largely due to his extensive "diaries" of Irving's activities and of events at the Lyceum Theatre. Stoker, who had no reason to believe that his own life would be worth remembering, devoted his diaries to documenting and preserving Irving's legacy.

SIGNED PHOTOGRAPH OF HENRY IRVING,
1895.
On loan from The Theatre Collection, Free Library of Philadelphia

KING ARTHUR
[broadside], Philadelphia, 30 December [1895].
On loan from The Theatre Collection, Free Library of Philadelphia

This broadside advertised the Lyceum Theatre's 1895 performance of J. Comyns Carr's *King Arthur* at Philadelphia's Chestnut Street Opera House. Henry Irving was in the title role, and Ellen Terry played Guinevere. Bram Stoker's name appears as acting manager.

NANCE OLDFIELD AND THE BELLS
[broadside], Philadelphia, 18 November 1901.
On loan from The Theatre Collection, Free Library of Philadelphia

The Bells, adapted from the French play *The Polish Jew* by Erckmann-Chatrian, was one of the Lyceum Theatre's greatest successes. Irving played the part of Mathias, who kills a Jew for his money and then is tormented by the sound of bells from the victim's sleigh. The role was a triumph for Irving, whose name would forever be associated with the part.

SIR HENRY IRVING AS CARDINAL WOLSEY
[postcard, n.d.].
On loan from The Theatre Collection, Free Library of Philadelphia

In 1892, Irving played the role of Cardinal Wolsey in the Lyceum Theatre's production of Shakespeare's *Henry VIII*.

AUTOGRAPH LETTER FROM STOKER TO AN UNKNOWN CORRESPONDENT.
Lyceum Theatre, London, 25 February 1891.

This letter is an example of the kind of correspondence Stoker handled as acting manager of the Lyceum Theatre. He writes: "Mr. Irving asks me to say that he is very sorry, but we are not playing *Ravenswood* [a dramatization of Sir Walter Scott's *Bride of Lammermoor*] till after Easter…. We play *Much Ado* tomorrow night…." Stoker encloses an article about Henry Irving.

WILLIAM SHAKESPEARE (1564–1616).
MACBETH
(London: C. Lowndes, 1794).

In December 1888, the Lyceum Theatre opened its first performance of *Macbeth*, one of the theater's most striking productions. Stoker admitted that this drama intrigued him more than any other. As he watched it performed at the Lyceum Theatre for 151 continuous performances, every line and nuance of the tragedy must have entered his consciousness. Many scholars have drawn parallels between *Macbeth* and *Dracula*. Both works feature dark, foreboding castles, sleepwalking scenes, pacts with supernatural forces, three witches (or in the case of *Dracula*, three seductive she-vampires), and many bloody deaths.

III Influences.

The legends that lie behind *Dracula* have a long literary ancestry, culminating in German *Sturm und Drang* and British romanticism. Stoker's Trinity education exposed him to works like Gottfried Bürger's "Lenore" and Goethe's "The Bride of Corinth," as well as Coleridge's "The Rime of the Ancient Mariner" and "Christabel," Robert Southey's "Thalaba the Destroyer," Keats's "La Belle Dame Sans Merci," and Byron's "The Giaour," all of which address the theme of life in death. The Gothic tales—Jane Austen's "horrid novels"—had created the popular image of sinister and supernatural happenings in Central Europe, reflected also in Sir Walter Scott's novels and poetry. In 1847, the year of Stoker's birth, James Malcolm Rymer's *Varney the Vampyre; or, The Feast of Blood* brought the adventures of an eighteenth-century aristocratic bloodsucker to Victorian England.

But contemporary works were also important influences, including Robert Louis Stevenson's *Strange Case of Dr. Jekyll and Mr. Hyde* (1886) and Oscar Wilde's *The Picture of Dorian Gray* (1891). The poems of Walt Whitman, which Stoker first read as a student at Trinity, had a dramatic impact, as did the poetry of Tennyson. But the most discernible sources are Sheridan Le Fanu's vampire story, "Carmilla," and Wilkie Collins's novels *The Woman in White* and *The Moonstone*. Le Fanu (1814–1873) was the greatest writer of supernatural fiction of his time. He was also a Dubliner, the editor and proprietor of the Dublin *Evening Mail*, in which Stoker's dramatic criticism appeared. *In a Glass Darkly*, a collection of his short stories including "Carmilla," was published in 1872. Like *Dracula*, *The Woman in White* (1860) is composed of letters, telegrams, and diary entries. In addition, Stoker's early notes for *Dracula*, which include a character identified as a "detective inspector," indicate that the novel was originally planned as a mystery or detective story.

> "You are a true man, and I would like to be one myself, and so I would be towards you as a brother and as a pupil to his master..."
>
> BRAM STOKER,
> in a letter to Walt Whitman,
> 18 February 1872

[JOHN WILLIAM POLIDORI (1795–1821).]
THE VAMPYRE
(London: Sherwood, Neely, and Jones, 1819).
On loan from the Department of Special Collections, Van-Pelt Dietrich Library, University of Pennsylvania

On a stormy night in June 1816 at the Villa Diodati on Lake Geneva, Percy Bysshe Shelley, Mary Shelley, Lord Byron, and Byron's personal physician, Dr. John Polidori, held a contest to determine who could write the most terrifying ghost story. Mary Shelley came up with a story that would become her classic novel, *Frankenstein*. Byron presented only a fragment of a tale; years later, Polidori resurrected Byron's idea, completed the story, and published it anonymously as *The Vampyre*. The work, originally attributed to Byron, was adapted for the stage by James Robinson Planché and performed at the Lyceum Theatre. Stoker must have been influenced by the character of Lord Ruthven, an elegant, aristocratic vampire who both seduces and terrifies his victims.

JOSEPH SHERIDAN LE FANU (1814–1873).
"CARMILLA."
From *In a Glass Darkly* (London: R. Bentley & Son, 1872). Volume 3.
On loan from the Fales Library, New York University

In 1872, Irish writer Sheridan Le Fanu published *In a Glass Darkly*, a collection of his short stories. The best known, "Carmilla," is a tale of lesbianism and vampirism featuring a she-vampire who preys on young maidens. Le Fanu's story was one of the first to emphasize the intense eroticism of the vampire's union with his or her victim. As she overtakes one of her conquests, Carmilla whispers:

> ...I live in your warm life, and you shall die—die, sweetly die—into mine. I cannot help it; as I draw near to you, you, in your turn will draw near to others, and learn the rapture of that cruelty, which is yet love...

As she is attacked, Carmilla's victim is repelled, yet fascinated: "I experienced a strange tumultuous excitement that was pleasurable, ever and anon, mingled with a vague sense of fear and disgust." Stoker drew from "Carmilla," especially in his early plans for the first two chapters of *Dracula,* which were later dropped from the published novel.

WALT WHITMAN (1819–1892).
"TRICKLE DROPS."
From *Leaves of Grass* (Camden, New Jersey: Author's edition, 1876).

While a student at Trinity, Stoker became a devotee of the poetry of Walt Whitman. In February 1872, he wrote a remarkable two-thousand word letter to Whitman but waited four years to mail it. The letter, one of the few that survive from Stoker's student days, is full of glowing appreciation for the poet's genius. The American tours of the Lyceum Theatre made it possible for Stoker to visit Whitman in Camden, New Jersey, whenever the troupe performed in Philadelphia. Stoker, accompanied by Henry Irving, first met Whitman in 1884; Stoker visited him again in 1886 and 1887.

According to Stoker's biographer Barbara Belford, Whitman had a profound impact on *Dracula.* His poetry celebrates the spiritual bonds between men and emphasizes the eroticism of death. In his poem "Trickle Drops," Whitman equates blood leaving the body with a sensual release:

> *Trickle, drops! my blue veins leaving!*
> *O drops of me! trickle, slow drops,*
> *Candid, from me falling—drip, bleeding drops,*
> *From wounds made to free you whence you were prison'd,*
> *From my face—from my forehead and lips,*
> *From my breast—from within where I was conceal'd*
> *—press forth, red drops—confession drops...*

SIGNED PHOTOGRAPH OF WALT WHITMAN, Philadelphia, 1882.

IV "Count Wampyr."

According to Noel Stoker, his father began writing *Dracula* after waking from a terrifying dream about a vampire king rising from the tomb. Noel's account was embraced by Stoker's earliest biographers, who claimed that the fateful nightmare was brought on by "a too generous helping of dressed crab at supper." Whatever inspired Stoker to begin the novel, a nightmare has always been at its center. Jonathan's dream of three vampire women seducing him in Dracula's castle was part of the plot from the very beginning, and Dracula's comment at the conclusion of the scene, "This man belongs to me," appears throughout Stoker's notes. Many critics interpret Dracula's statement as evidence of his sexual attraction to Jonathan.

Stoker began preparing an outline for *Dracula* as early as March 1890, seven years before the novel was published. He continued to work on other projects during that time, completing three adventure/romance novels: *The Snake's Pass* (1891), *The Watter's Mou'* (1895), and *The Shoulder of Shasta* (1895). It is remarkable that Stoker found the time to write, given his overwhelming responsibilities at the Lyceum Theatre, but his background in journalism had trained him to write quickly, and he rarely prepared more than two drafts of a work.

Despite his tendency to dash off a short story during a free hour or a book during a summer vacation, Stoker crafted his vampire novel with a very different approach. The work consumed him; he was obsessed with every detail, from train schedules to Transylvanian costume. He strived for accuracy and authenticity at every turn, taking

> *"I suppose I must have fallen asleep; I hope so, but I fear, for all that followed was startlingly real—so real that now, sitting here in the broad, full sunlight of the morning, I cannot in the least believe that it was all sleep."*
>
> JONATHAN HARKER, *Dracula,* Chapter 3

Stoker's earliest notes for *Dracula*, March 1890
[*Notes*, page 35 verso a]

careful notes, planning every plot twist in advance, and revising the story line numerous times. Unlike his other novels, *Dracula* was a long-term project that took seven years to complete.

[OUTLINE FOR CHAPTER I OF DRACULA],
8 MARCH 1890.
[page 35 verso a]
Stoker's earliest notes for *Dracula*, an outline of the opening chapters, are dated 8 March 1890. The notes reveal that the Count's castle was originally located in Styria, a region in southeastern Austria (the same setting as Le Fanu's vampire story, "Carmilla"). Remarkably, seven years before the publication of *Dracula*, Stoker had already outlined the scene describing Jonathan Harker's dream in Dracula's castle: "man goes out sees girls one tries to kiss him not on lips but throat. Old Count interferes—rage & fury diabolical—this man belongs to me I want him."

[OUTLINES FOR BOOK I, CHAPTERS I AND 2, BETWEEN 1890 AND 1896].
[pages 5 and 6]
These outlines for Chapters 1 and 2 summarize the purchase of the Count's property in England and recount the experiences of Jonathan Harker as he travels to Styria, stopping in Munich to view a performance of Wagner's *The Flying Dutchman* (Henry Irving frequently played the leading role in *Vanderdecken*, a play based on the Flying Dutchman legend). At this early stage, Stoker calls his vampire "Count Wampyr"; it would be several months before he discovered and settled on the name "Dracula." In the notes, Stoker originally writes "Count Wampyr"; at a later date, he crosses out "Wampyr" and replaces it with "Dracula."

DRACULA'S GUEST AND OTHER WEIRD STORIES
(London: George Routledge & Sons, 1914).
On loan from the Bram Stoker Memorial Association, New York
Early versions of the first two chapters for *Dracula* were cut from the novel before it was published. The work is stronger without these opening scenes, which borrow elements from other works. After Stoker's death, his widow published a collection of his short fiction entitled *Dracula's Guest and Other Weird Stories* (1914). Shown here is a rare example of the first edition, with its dust jacket still intact. The abandoned idea for the second chapter of *Dracula* resurfaces in the book as a short story called "Dracula's Guest."

[OUTLINE FOR BOOKS I–IV OF DRACULA],
14 MARCH 1890.
[page 2]
By mid-March 1890, Stoker had completed an outline for *Dracula*, which he divided into four books: "Styria to London" (he later crossed out Styria and inserted "Transylvania"), "Tragedy," "Discovery," and "Punishment." Many scholars suggest that Stoker's division of the novel resembles four acts of a play, each with seven scenes, further evidence that he had a theatrical production in mind while writing *Dracula*.

[EARLY LIST OF CHARACTERS, BETWEEN 1890 AND 1896].
[page 35a]
At the time he recorded this early list of characters for *Dracula*, Stoker had selected types, but not names, of people to be included in the book. He lists "Lawyer's clerk" (Jonathan Harker), "Mad Doctor—loves girl" (Dr. Seward), "Mad patient" who has a "theory of perpetual life" (Renfield), and "Girl—dies" (Lucy Westenra). Stoker also lists "Philosophic historian," "German professor of history," and "Detective inspector," three characters who were later combined into the character of Dr. Van Helsing.

"HISTORIAE PERSONAE," [BETWEEN 1890 AND 1896].
[page 1]
This list contains many of the characters who appear in *Dracula*, as well as several who were later dropped. Included is "Doctor of Madhouse" (Dr. Seward), Lucy Westenra, the "Mad Patient" (Renfield), Peter Hawkins, Jonathan Harker, Mina Murray, a "German Professor" named Max Windshoeffel (who later becomes the Dutch professor, Dr. Van Helsing), and a Texan named "Brutus M. Moris" (who is later called Quincey P. Morris). The Count originally appears as "Count Wampyr"; at a later date, Stoker crosses out "Wampyr" and inserts "Dracula." He writes "Dracula" twice at the top of the page and then, in the top-left corner, writes and firmly underlines "Count Dracula." Stoker had finally settled on a name for his infamous vampire.

Book I.
Styria to London

- Chap 1 — The lawyers letters &c
- " 2 — (Clerk visit Transylvania) Munich
- " 3 — the Journey — wolves — blue flame &c
- " 4 — Arrival the Castle
- " 5 — Loneliness the Kiss "this man belongs to me"
- " 6 — old chapel Carrying earth. Sortes Virgiliana (notes in letter)
- " 7 — The warehouse of London estate Dr Seward's diary — fly patient — loved down

Book II
Tragedy

- Chap 1 — The auctioneer Whitby — argument uncanny things
- " 2 — The Doctor Whitby — the storm — ship arrives
- " 3 — The Lawyers Clerk Whitby — they walk in sleep — Lucy
- " 4 — A night of Terror London Mina's wedding
- " 5 — A medical impasse A night of Terror (wolf rising) Dracula visits asylum
- " 6 — The tragedy a medical impasse Lucy dies
- " 7 — The vow Opening vault. The Vow

Book III
Discovery

- Chap 1 — The suspicion — Harker's diary
- " 2 — Inquiries — the Dunes — re Vampires
- " 3 — Mina enlists Dracula Travels to Transylvania
- " 4 — On the track Texan in Transylvania
- " 5 — Strange clues — Count's house searched bloodred room
- " 6 — a test of sanity (?)
- " 7 — Conviction Harker sees the Count

Book IV
Punishment

- Chap 1 — The Dunes of thirteen
- " 2 — a Vigilante Committee
- " 3 — Desufferance
- " 4 — a choice of dwellings
- " 5 — Closing the net (removing earth).
- " 6 — Back to Styria Transylvania
- " 7 — a Tourists Tale

Dying in the Texan   (Cowhilled & wolf welts?)

Count Dracula.

Dracula ~~Historiæ~~ Personal   Dracula
_____

o Doctor of madhouse ~~~~ ~~~~ Seward
   Girl engaged to him Lucy Westenra schoolfellow of Miss Murray
o Mad Patient (theory of getting life — instinctively goes for Count & follows
                 up idea with mad cunning.
o Lawer ~~Arthur abbott~~ John Peter Hawkins Exet.
o His clerk ———————— Jonathan Harker
o Fiancée of above ~~~~ Wilhelmina Murray (called Mina)
   ~~~~ ~~~~
   ~~her sister~~
o ~~~~ schoolfellow of above ———— Kate Reed
   The Count ———— Count ~~Wampyr~~ Dracula
   A ~~Deaf~~ Mute woman } helping
   A Silent Man   } servants of
                              the Count
o A Detective ———————————— Cotford
o A Psychical Research Agent ———— Alfred Singleton
   ~~An American inventor from Texas~~
o A German Professor ———— Max Windshoeffel
o A Painter ———— Francis Aytown
o A Texan ———— Brutus M. Marix

   o makes dinner of 13   Mem
                         secret room — ~~~~ like blood

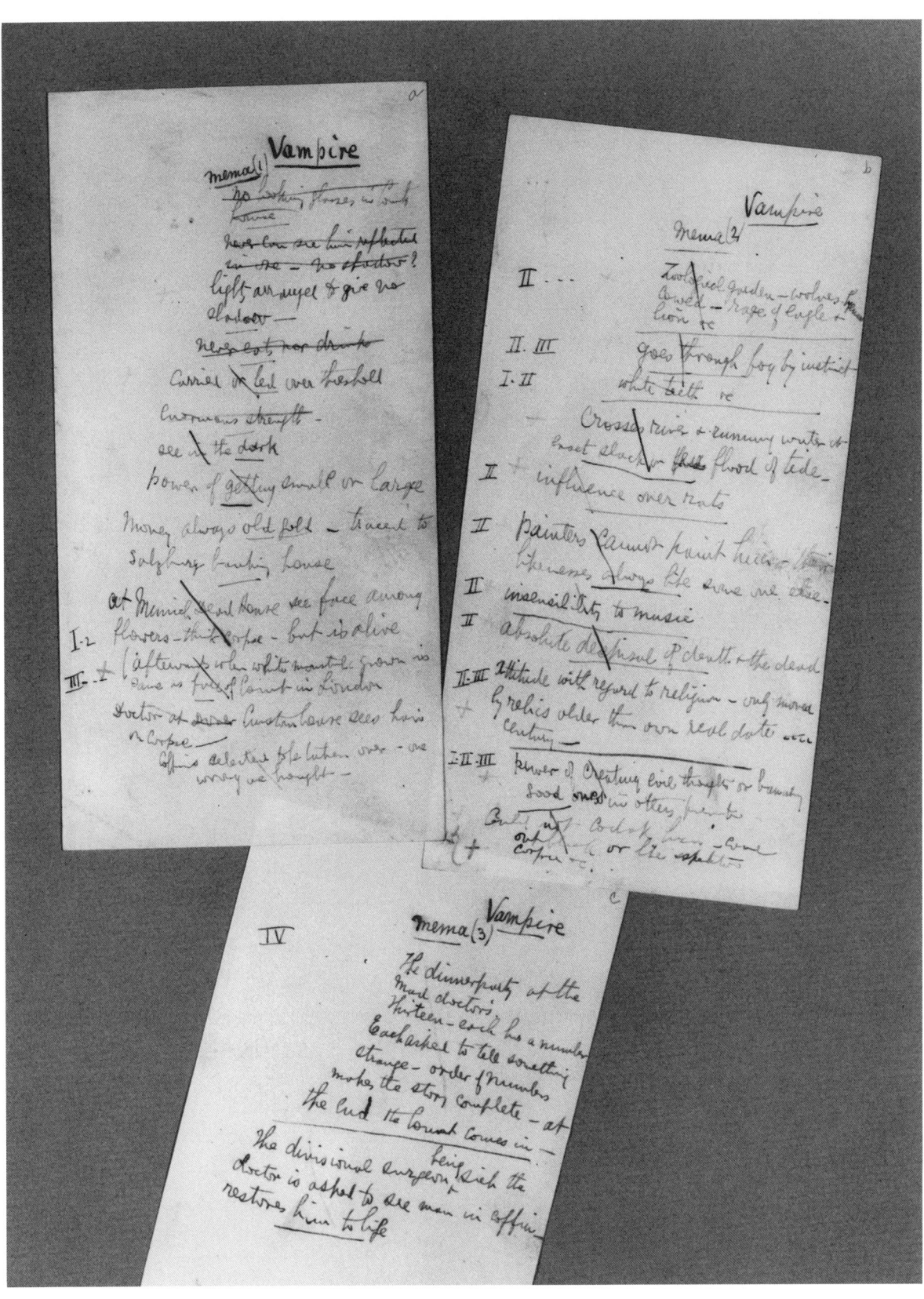

Stoker's list of vampire characteristics
[Notes, pages 38a, 38b, and 38c]

[LIST OF VAMPIRE CHARACTERISTICS, BETWEEN 1890 AND 1896].

[page 4]

After developing his list of characters, Stoker began assembling the traits of his anti-hero, Dracula. Although he drew upon traditional vampire legends and literature, Stoker also invented new vampire characteristics, such as "influence over rats; painters cannot reproduce him ... insensible to music ... power of creating evil thoughts & destroying will ... can see in the dark ..."

[LIST OF VAMPIRE CHARACTERISTICS, BETWEEN 1890 AND 1896].

[pages 38a, 38b, and 38c]

These pages of notes include some of the vampire qualities mentioned above as well as additional characteristics. Stoker writes: "no looking glasses in Count's house; never can see him reflected in one—no shadow? ... never eats nor drinks ... enormous strength ... money always old gold ..." As he did frequently throughout his notes, Stoker put a mark through each trait as he used it in the novel.

On the third page, Stoker describes a dinner party for thirteen people hosted by the "Mad Doctor" (Dr. Seward). According to Stoker's notes, one guest starts a "strange" story that is continued by the next guest, and so on, until every guest has added to the tale. At the end of the story, "the Count comes in." This intriguing scene does not appear in the novel.

SABINE BARING-GOULD (1834–1924). BOOK OF WERE-WOLVES
(London: Smith Elder, 1865). Mrs. Sabine Baring-Gould's copy.

On loan from The Book Sail, Orange, California

In addition to vampires, Stoker considered other supernatural creatures as he fleshed out his character of Count Dracula. He consulted the *Book of Were-Wolves* by Sabine Baring-Gould, a well-known writer on folklore, to learn more about these "children of the night." While reading this work, Stoker might have seen a reference to Elizabeth Báthory, a sixteenth-century Hungarian countess who bathed in the blood of virgins to maintain her youthful appearance.

[NOTES FROM SABINE BARING-GOULD'S BOOK OF WERE-WOLVES], [BETWEEN 1890 AND 1896].

[page 43 verso a]

In his notes from Baring-Gould's book, Stoker lists several werewolf characteristics: "canine teeth protruding over lower lip when mouth closed [like] pointed nails ... short fingers & has some hairs in hollow of hand...." In the novel, Dracula is described as having many of these qualities:

[He had] peculiarly sharp white teeth; these protruded over the lips ... [his hands] were rather coarse—broad, with squat fingers. Strange to say, there were hairs in the centre of the palm.

The idea of Dracula as a werewolf is emphasized in Chapter 7 of the novel, when he springs from the shipwrecked *Demeter* in the form of a wild dog.

V Whitby.

In the summer of 1890, Bram, Florence, and Noel Stoker vacationed in Whitby, a popular seaside resort in Yorkshire, on the coast of northeastern England. During this family holiday, Stoker recorded observations of the town's geography, weather conditions, architecture, and people. Later, he selected the town as the vacation destination for Mina Murray and Lucy Westenra, setting several chapters of *Dracula* there. Stoker's detailed notes provide authenticity for this section of the novel, in which Whitby and its inhabitants play a major role.

Stoker also selected Whitby as the location of the fateful shipwreck that brings Count Dracula from Eastern Europe to the shores of England. The shipwreck in the novel is based on an event that occurred in October 1885, when a ferocious storm

"This is a lovely place."
MINA MURRAY,
Dracula, Chapter 6

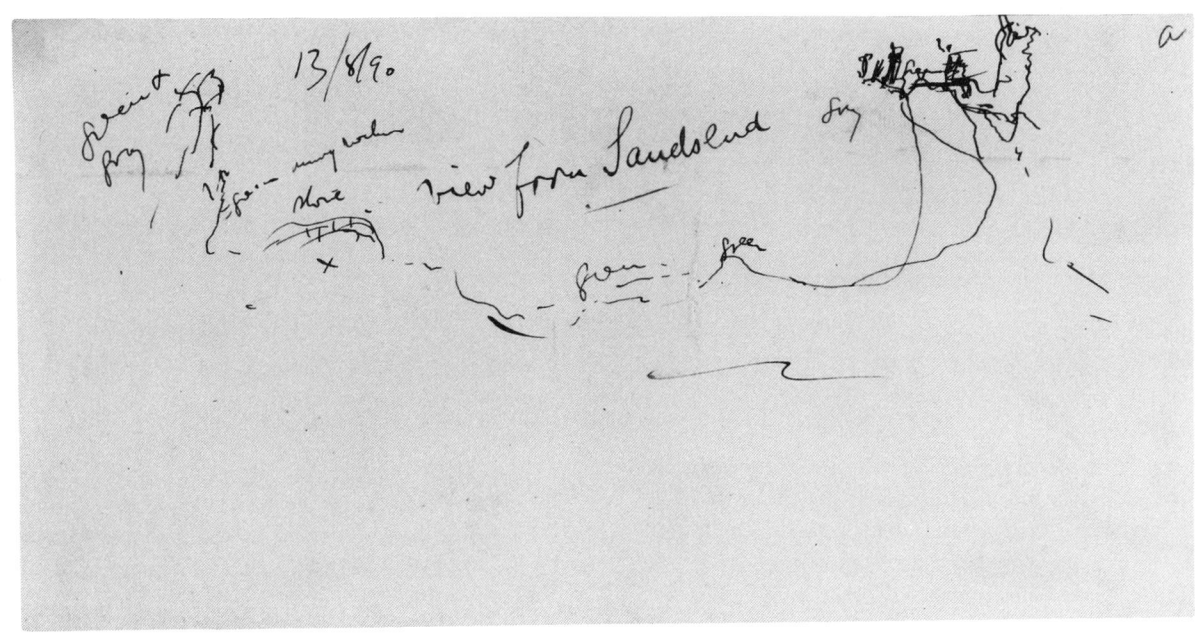

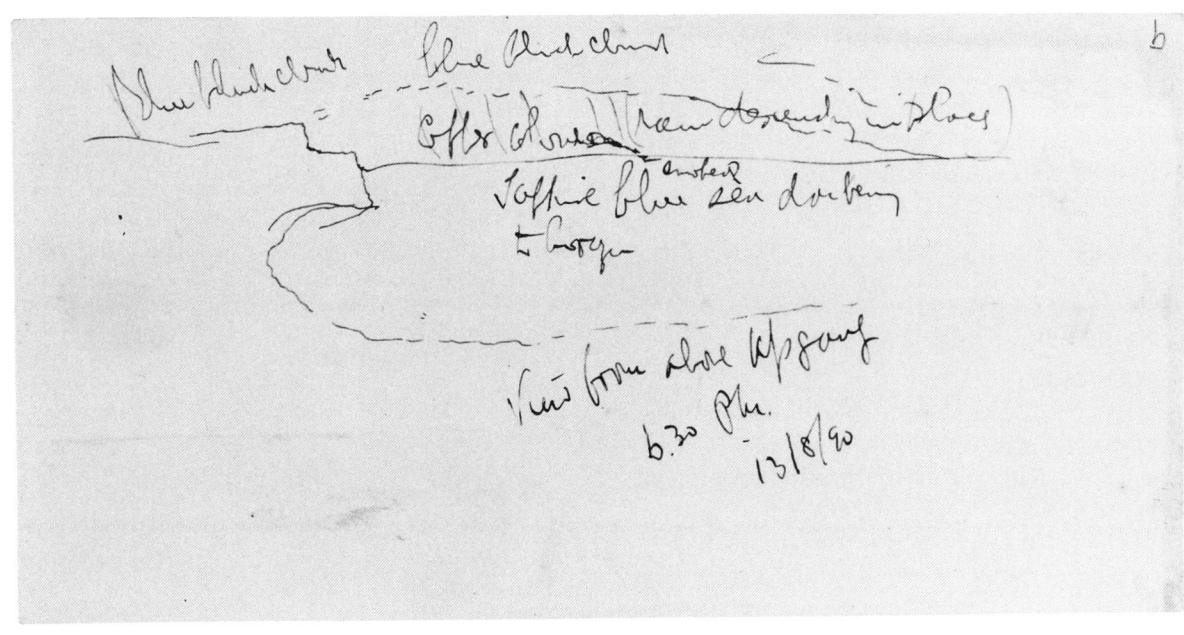

Stoker's sketches of Whitby, August 1890
[Notes, pages 47 verso a and 47 verso b]

tossed the Russian schooner *Dimitry* onto the shore. After learning about the shipwreck from a Coast Guardsman, Stoker went to the Whitby Library to study accounts of the event in local newspapers.

HORNE'S GUIDE TO WHITBY, PROFUSELY ILLUSTRATED
(Whitby: Horne & Son, 1895).
On loan from the Bram Stoker Memorial Association, New York

[NOTES ON WEATHER CONDITIONS IN WHITBY], 11 AUGUST 1890.
[page 42 verso a]
Stoker reproduced some of his Whitby notes almost verbatim in *Dracula*. As he observed the Whitby weather on August 11, he wrote: "grey day—sun high over Kettleness—all grey ... grey earthy rock ... grey clouds tinged with sunburst ... all vastness—clouds piled up & a 'brool' over the sea—like a presage—dark figures on beach here & there—men like trees walking...." In *Dracula*, Mina Murray records an almost identical description of the Whitby weather:

To-day is a grey day, and the sun as I write is hidden in thick clouds, high over Kettleness. Everything is grey ... grey earthy rock; grey clouds, tinged with the sunburst at the far edge, hang over the grey sea ... All is vastness; the clouds are piled up like giant rocks, and there is a "brool" over the sea that sounds like some presage of doom. Dark figures are on the beach here and there, sometimes half shrouded in the mist, and seem "men like trees walking."

"VIEW FROM SANDSEND" AND "VIEW FROM ABOVE UPGANG," WHITBY, 13 AUGUST 1890.
[pages 47 verso a and 47 verso b]
Stoker sketched various scenes in Whitby to ensure that he had recorded every detail of the landscape accurately. These sketches feature the "view from Sandsend" (a small village west of Whitby) and the "view from above Upgang" (a steep path leading up from the beach). In the second drawing, Stoker depicts the "blue black clouds" hanging over the "saffire [sic] blue sea..."

"GLOSSARY—WHITBY" [AUGUST 1890?].
[pages 41a and 41b]
During his vacation, Stoker enjoyed consorting with local fisherman and listening to their tales. He made a point to understand, record, and "translate" their dialect; in fact, he consulted Francis Kildale Robinson's *A Glossary of Words Used in the Neighbourhood of Whitby* (1876) and copied out a list of words in the Whitby dialect. Stoker used the dialect in Chapter 6 of *Dracula*, when Mina and Lucy converse with the Whitby locals.

"TOMBSTONES—WHITBY CHURCHYARD ON CLIFF" [AUGUST 1890?].
[pages 76, 77, and 81]
While in Whitby, Stoker recorded more than eighty inscriptions from the tombstones in St. Mary's churchyard; these notes were later copied onto ten typewritten pages. The inscriptions are ridiculed in an extended passage from Chapter 6 of *Dracula*, when Mina and Lucy sit in the churchyard with Mr. Swales, a Whitby local. In his nearly incomprehensible dialect, Swales proclaims that the tombstone inscriptions are all lies:

... 'Here lies the body' or 'Sacred to the memory' wrote on all of them, an' yet in nigh half of them there bean't no bodies at all [because they were lost at sea]; an' the memories of them bean't cared a pinch of snuff about, much less sacred. Lies all of them, nothin' but lies of one kind or another!

To prove his point, Swales cites the inscriptions on the tombstones of Edward Spencelagh, Braithwaite Lowrey, Andrew Woodhouse, and John Paxton, names Stoker copied directly from the tombstones. A tombstone was also the source of Mr. Swales's name.

[NOTES ON WHITBY SHIPWRECK], 11 AUGUST 1890.
[page 42b]
On the evening of August 11, Stoker spoke with William Petherick, a Whitby Coast Guardsman. In his notes from that conversation, Stoker wrote: "Told me of various wrecks. A Russian schooner 120 tons from Black Sea ran in with all sails...." Stoker was fascinated by the tale and incorporated it into *Dracula*. What more dramatic an entrance for the Count than to arrive in England on a ship that strikes the Yorkshire coast?

"DETAIL OF WRECKS AT WHITBY,"
24 OCTOBER 1885.
[page 40 verso]
Although Stoker based the fictional shipwreck in *Dracula* on the wreck of the *Dimitry*, he altered the details of that event and changed the name of the Russian schooner to the *Demeter*. This account of the wreck of the *Dimitry* reports that the crew survived the storm and were brought safely to shore. In the novel, the *Demeter* washes ashore with only dead bodies aboard; Dracula has fed on and killed the entire crew. Stoker adds an additional horrifying detail when he describes the lifeless body of the Russian captain lashed to the helm.

FRANK M. SUTCLIFF (1853-1941).
[PHOTOGRAPH OF THE RUSSIAN SCHOONER DIMITRY ON THE WHITBY COAST, OCTOBER 1885].
Stoker viewed this haunting photograph of the *Dimitry* while conducting research in the Whitby Library. The photographer, Frank Sutcliff, earned an international reputation for his photographs of Whitby and its inhabitants during the nineteenth century. Sutcliff's powerful image of the schooner precariously beached on the shore provided visual inspiration for Stoker's description of the shipwreck in *Dracula*.

VI Transylvania.

Before writing *Dracula*, Stoker consulted numerous secondary sources and took detailed notes, many of which survive. While on holiday in Whitby, he spent hours in the local library, and after returning to London, he continued his research in the British Library. One of Stoker's challenges was that part of the novel was set in Transylvania, a region he had never visited. After *Dracula* was published, an American journalist criticized Stoker for describing distant lands he had never seen; the author coolly replied: "Trees are trees, mountains are, generally speaking, mountains, no matter in what country you find them, and one description may be made to answer for all."

Despite his flippant response to the American journalist, Stoker made every effort to describe Transylvania accurately. To familiarize himself with the region's history, geography, language, and customs, he consulted a number of works, including A. F. Crosse's *Round About the Carpathians* (1878), Major E. C. Johnson's *On the Track of the Crescent* (1885), Charles Boner's *Transylvania* (1865), William Wilkinson's *Account of the Principalities of Wallachia and Moldavia* (1820), and Emily de Laszkowski Gerard's *The Land Beyond the Forest* (1888). At some point, many of Stoker's research notes were typed up on a very early typewriter; they contain extensive corrections and additions, probably in his hand.

"Having had some time at my disposal when in London, I had visited the British Museum, and made search among the books and maps in the library regarding Transylvania; it had struck me that some foreknowledge of the country could hardly fail to have some importance in dealing with a nobleman of that country."

JONATHAN HARKER,
Dracula, Chapter 1

[NOTES FROM AN ACCOUNT OF THE PRINCIPALITIES OF WALLACHIA AND MOLDAVIA], [AUGUST 1890?].
[page 71]
While in the Whitby Library, Stoker consulted William Wilkinson's *Account of the Principalities of Wallachia and Moldavia*. Wilkinson's book might have provided Stoker with his first exposure to the word "Dracula." He copied out this passage from a footnote on page 19:

Dracula in Wallachian language means Devil. Wallachians were accustomed to give it as a surname to any person who rendered himself conspicuous by courage, cruel actions or cunning.

The book also contained information on the historical figure Vlad Tepes, who ruled Wallachia, now part of Romania, from 1456 to 1462. Vlad was known as "Vlad the Impaler," a reference to his preferred means of executing his enemies; he was also called "Dracole" or "Dracula."

ACCOUNT OF THE PRINCIPALITIES OF WALLACHIA AND MOLDAVIA, ETC. *1820*
Wm. Wilkinson late consul of Bukorest. Longmans. Whitby Library. O.1097.

/

P.19. DRACULA in Wallachian language means DEVIL. Wallachians were accustomed to give it as a surname to any person who rendered himself conspicuous by courage, cruel actions or cunning.

P.18.19. The Wallachians joined Hungarians in 1448. and made war on Turkey, being defeated at battle of Cassova in Bulgaria and finding it impossible to make stand against the Turks submitted to annual tribute which they paid until 1460. when Sultan Mahomet II. being occupied in completing conquest of islands in Archipelogo gave opportunity of shaking off yoke. Their VOIVODE [DRACULA] crossed Danube and attacked Turkish troops Only momentarily success. Mahomet drove him back to Wallachia where pursued and defeated him. The VOIVODE escaped into Hungary and the Sultan caused his brother *Bladus* retired in his place. He made treaty with Bladus finding Wallachians to *perpetual* tribute and laid the foundations of that slavery not yet abolished. [1820]

Notes from William Wilkinson's *Account of the Principalities of Wallachia and Moldavia*, where Stoker might have seen the word "Dracula" for the first time
[Notes, page 71]

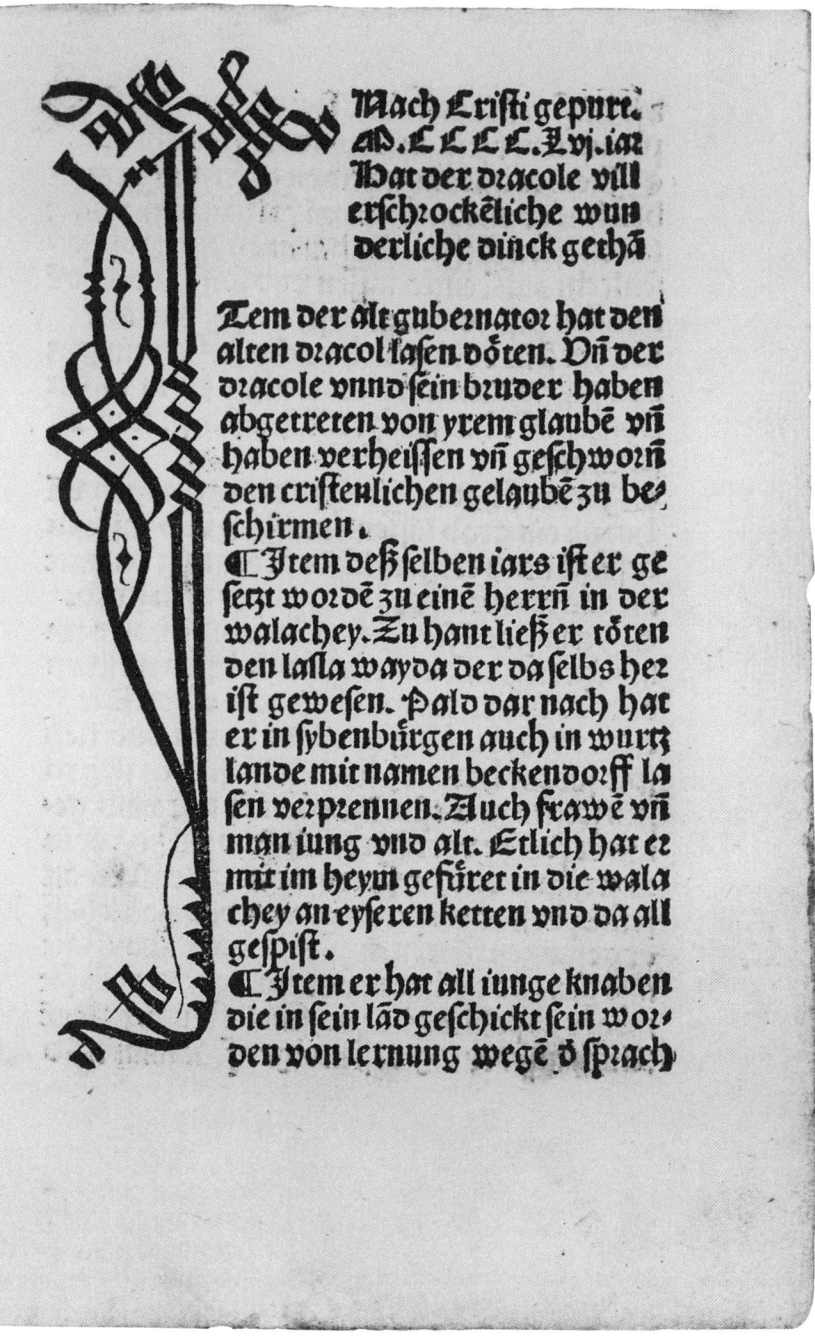

Nach Cristi gepurt
M.CCCC.Lvj. iar
hat der dracole vill
erschrockeliche wun
derliche dinck gethā

Item der alt gubernator hat den
alten dracol lasen döten. Vñ der
dracole vnnd sein bruder haben
abgetreten von yrem glaubē vñ
haben verheissen vñ geschworn
den cristenlichen gelaubē zu be
schirmen.

Item deß selben iars ist er ge
setzt wordē zu einē herrn in der
walachey. Zu hant ließ er töten
den lasla wayda der da selbs her
ist gewesen. Pald dar nach hat
er in sybenbürgen auch in wurtz
lande mit namen beckendorff la
sen verprennen. Auch frawē vñ
man iung vnd alt. Etlich hat er
mit im heym gefüret in die wala
chey an eyseren ketten vnd da all
gespist.

Item er hat all iunge knaben
die in sein lad geschickt sein wor
den von lernung wegē ð sprach

First text page from *Dracole Waida*

DRACOLE WAIDA
(Nuremberg, 1488).

Perhaps inspired by what he had discovered about Vlad Tepes in Whitby, Stoker went to the British Library to learn more about the ruthless ruler known as "Dracula." Here he consulted a German pamphlet, published in Bamberg in 1491, describing Vlad's exploits. The pamphlet included a woodcut portrait of Vlad with long, curly hair and a heavy mustache and eyebrows. This woodcut might have provided Stoker with some of Dracula's physical characteristics. In the novel, the Count is described as having a "long white mustache" and "hair growing scantily round the temples, but profusely elsewhere. His eyebrows were very massive, almost meeting over the nose, and with bushy hair that seemed to curl in its own profusion."

The Rosenbach's *Dracole Waida* (1488), the only copy held in an American library, is a slightly earlier version of the pamphlet Stoker consulted in the British Library. The woodcut of Vlad Tepes in the Rosenbach copy, which is similar to the one found in the 1491 Bamberg edition, was hand-painted during the fifteenth century.

EMILY DE LASZKOWSKI GERARD (1849–1905).
THE LAND BEYOND THE FOREST
(Edinburgh and London: W. Blackwood & Sons, 1888).
On loan from the Athenaeum of Philadelphia

Emily Gerard, the English wife of a commander in the Hungarian cavalry, was fascinated by the folklore and superstitions of Transylvania, where she lived with her husband for two years. She recorded her observations in the 1888 publication *The Land Beyond the Forest* (a translation of "Transylvania"), in which she wrote: "It would almost seem as though the whole species of demons, pixies, witches, and hobgoblins, driven from the rest of Europe by the wand of science, had taken refuge within this mountain rampart." Stoker was familiar with Gerard's book, which might have inspired him to locate Dracula's castle in Transylvania, rather than Styria. He included many Transylvanian superstitions in the novel, such as the mysterious blue flames that Jonathan Harker observes during his coach ride to Dracula's castle. According to Gerard, blue flames indicated the location of buried treasure.

[NOTES FROM EMILY GERARD'S "TRANSYLVANIAN SUPERSTITIONS," XIX CENTURY, VOL. XVIII, JULY 1885, PP. 130–50], [BETWEEN 1890 AND 1896].
[pages 38 verso a and 39a]

Stoker also read and took notes from Emily Gerard's article "Transylvanian Superstitions," which describes several methods for killing vampires. In his notes from the article, Stoker writes: "to kill vampire drive stake through corpse or fire pistol shot into coffin or cut off head & replace in coffin with mouth full of garlic or extract heart & burn it & strew ashes over grave."

SIR WILLIAM THORNLEY STOKER (1845–1912). [MEMORANDUM ON HEAD INJURIES, BETWEEN 1890 AND 1896].
[page 45]

This memorandum describing the medical effects of a severe blow to the head was written by Stoker's older brother, Thornley, a prominent physician and President of the Royal College of Surgeons in Ireland. Stoker used this information in Chapter 21 of *Dracula*, when he describes the extensive injuries suffered by Renfield, the mad patient in Dr. Seward's insane asylum. Renfield receives his injuries at the hands of Count Dracula, who enters his cell by turning himself into mist.

"VAMPIRES IN NEW ENGLAND." NEW YORK WORLD, 2 FEBRUARY 1896.
[page 46 verso]

Stoker might have clipped this article from the *New York World* during the Lyceum Theatre's American tour of 1896. The article focuses on vampire superstitions in Rhode Island, where "people have been digging up the dead bodies of relatives for the purpose of burning their hearts.... Not merely the out-of-the-way agricultural folk, but the more intelligent people of the urban communities are strong in their belief in vampirism." Stoker must have been delighted to discover that the topic of his soon-to-be-released novel was making headlines in an American newspaper.

VII The Vampire Novel.

Eventually, Stoker's careful planning and research began to bear fruit. As he pulled together scraps of paper containing his notes, outlines, and lists, his vampire novel took shape. In February 1892, Stoker drafted a revised outline for the novel and began plotting the action in each chapter. These chapter outlines are sketchy, yet evocative; Stoker uses phrases and words strung together with dashes to indicate the mood and events in each scene. Although the plot of the completed novel closely follows the chapter outlines, there are many significant differences, indicating that Stoker continued to revise the novel during the next five years.

> "In this matter dates are everything, and I think that if we get all our material ready, and have every item put in chronological order, we shall have done much."
>
> MINA HARKER,
> *Dracula*, Chapter 17

[CALENDAR OF EVENTS IN DRACULA, BETWEEN 1890 AND 1896].
[pages 27a and 29a]
Stoker's notes for *Dracula* reveal the author's almost obsessive attention to detail. These leaves demonstrate that he carefully plotted the daily action of the novel on a desk calendar. The days and dates listed on the calendar reveal that the novel is set in the year 1893, corresponding with Stoker's comment that he wanted *Dracula* to take place in present-day England, which, for Stoker, would have been the early 1890s.

[NOTES ON TRAIN SCHEDULES, BETWEEN 1890 AND 1896].
[pages 36b and 36c]
These notes on train schedules outline Jonathan Harker's journey at the beginning of *Dracula*. He travels by train from London to Klausenberg, then by coach from Klausenberg to the Borgo Pass. Again, Stoker insisted on using authentic train schedules, probably finding them in *Baedeker's Southern Germany and Austria, Including Hungary and Transylvania* (1880). Stoker made all travel arrangements for the Lyceum Theatre and was familiar both with complicated train schedules and *Baedeker's* guides.

[OUTLINE FOR DRACULA], 29 FEBRUARY 1892.
[page 35 verso b]
By February 1892, Stoker had prepared a revised outline for *Dracula*. In his first outline, dated March 1890, the novel was in four parts, each with seven chapters. In this outline, prepared two years later, Stoker divides the book into three parts with nine chapters each. The published book, which is not divided into parts, has the same number of total chapters (twenty-seven). At this point, Stoker still had not selected names for Quincey P. Morris or Renfield; they are referred to as the "Texan" and the "flyman."

[OUTLINE FOR CHAPTER 3 OF DRACULA, BETWEEN 1890 AND 1896].
[page 7]
What Stoker originally planned as Chapter 3 of *Dracula* eventually became the opening chapter of the novel, describing Jonathan Harker's journey to Dracula's castle. In his outline, Stoker provides a vivid list of Jonathan's experiences:

... the journey wolves howl & surround—blue flames—driver stops—knife thrown & strange sounds—mist—thunder—dogs & wolves howl—midnight arrival at castle—describe—left alone—enter Count [—] supper—to bed—describe room etc...

Stoker's "enter Count" reads like a stage direction for Henry Irving.

[OUTLINE FOR CHAPTER 6 OF DRACULA, BETWEEN 1890 AND 1896].
[page 10]
This outline contains a scene that was later dropped from the novel. Stoker describes Jonathan's encounter with wolves and a werewolf after his escape from Dracula's castle:

Attempt to get away from Castle—Wolves—wehr wolf old chapel—carting earth—shrieks from grave—sights of terror etc. falling senseless, found by Count. Is it all a dream [—] back to London

In Stoker's notes, Jonathan returns to London immediately; in the novel, he escapes to a convent in Budapest, recovers from his trauma, and is later joined by Mina.

[OUTLINE FOR CHAPTER 26 OF DRACULA, BETWEEN 1890 AND 1896].
[page 34]
Stoker worked on *Dracula* whenever he had the opportunity, even when the Lyceum Theatre was touring the United States. He wrote his outline for Chapter 26 on the letterhead of Philadelphia's Stratford Hotel (now the Bellevue Hotel) on Broad and Walnut Streets. Stoker stayed in the hotel during one of the Lyceum Theatre's visits to Philadelphia.

Stoker's outline for Chapter 26, on the letterhead of Philadelphia's Stratford Hotel
[Notes, page 34]

VIII "The Un=Dead."

A handwritten manuscript for *Dracula* has never been found. It is possible that Stoker skipped the manuscript stage altogether and went directly from his handwritten notes to a typescript of the novel. The typescript for *Dracula*, owned by a private collector, contains extensive corrections and emendations by Stoker, his brother Thornley, and an editor. Clearly, major revisions were still occurring at this stage, indicating that the typescript might have come directly from the notes, without an intermediary handwritten manuscript.

Although it is hard to imagine Stoker's classic vampire novel by any other name, *Dracula* was not his first choice for a title. In fact, the work was originally called *The Un-Dead*, which appears on the first page of the typescript. On 20 May 1897, when Stoker signed the contract with his publisher, the novel was still entitled *The Un-Dead*. Yet, just six days later, when the work appeared in bookstores, it was called *Dracula*. It is unclear why the title was changed at the last minute.

On 18 May 1897, eight days before *Dracula* became available to the public, Stoker organized a staged reading of the novel at the Lyceum Theatre. This five-hour pre-publication performance secured his dramatic rights to the book and allowed him to expose the work to Henry Irving. According to legend, when Irving was asked what he thought, he replied, "Dreadful!" Thus, much to Stoker's disappointment, Irving never played the part of Dracula, nor did any other actor during Stoker's lifetime. Perhaps Irving objected to the fact that Count Dracula is offstage so much of the time; he appears on only sixty-two pages of the 360-page novel. Clearly, the great actor would not have considered playing a part that allowed him to be on stage for only one-sixth of the play.

"She was bitten by the vampire when she was in a trance.... In trance she died, and in trance she is Un-Dead, too.... When they become such, there comes with the change the curse of immortality; they cannot die, but must go on age after age adding new victims and multiplying the evils of the world; for all that die from the preying of the Un-Dead become themselves Un-Dead ..."

DR. VAN HELSING,
Dracula, Chapters 15 and 16

[LIST OF CHARACTERS IN DRACULA, BETWEEN 1890 AND 1896].
[page 31b verso]

This list of characters was probably prepared sometime near the completion of the novel. Arthur Holmwood appears for the first time, and the Texan is listed as "Quincey P. Adams," who would eventually become Quincey P. Morris. Perhaps the most important detail in these notes, however, is Stoker's memorandum on the right, where he lists two possible titles for his vampire novel: *The Un-Dead* or *The Dead Un-Dead*.

THE UN-DEAD
[typescript], Chapter 1, page 1, [ca. 1896].
On loan from The Book Sail, Orange, California

THE UN-DEAD
[typescript], Chapter 27, page 539, [ca. 1896].
On loan from The Book Sail, Orange, California

Stoker's typescript for *The Un-Dead* reveals that he at first envisioned a rather different ending for the novel. Originally, Dracula's castle is destroyed in a volcanic eruption after he is killed by Jonathan Harker and Quincey P. Morris. However, this passage, describing the explosion, is crossed out from the typescript:

As we looked there came a terrible convulsion of the earth so that we seemed to rock to and fro and fell to our knees. At the same moment with a roar which seemed to shake the very heavens the

Count Drakulya
Peter Hawkins
Jonathan Harker
Mina Murray
Sir Robert Parton
John Seward
Quincey P. Adams
Hon Arthur Holmwood son of Viscount Godalming
Dr Van Helsing
Mrs Westenra
Lucy Westenra
Dr Vincent: North Hospital

Mem
novel. The Un-Dead —
    or
The Dead Un-Dead. —

A final list of characters, with Stoker's memorandum on possible titles for his vampire novel
[Notes, page 31b verso]

whole castle and the rock and even the hill on which it stood seemed to rise into the air and scatter in fragments while a mighty cloud of black and yellow smoke volume on volume in rolling grandeur was shot upwards with inconceivable rapidity.... From where we stood it seemed as though the one fierce volcano burst had satisfied the need of nature and that the castle and the structure of the hill had sunk again into the void.

Some critics suggest that the ending of *Dracula* was changed because it was too similar to the conclusion of Edgar Allan Poe's "The Fall of the House of Usher." It seems likely, however, that the passage was deleted to leave open the possibility of a sequel, with Dracula returning from the grave to reinhabit his castle and wreak vengeance on his enemies.

IX "Dracula."

Dracula appeared in bookstores on 26 May 1897. The first edition of three thousand copies must have disappointed Stoker; its yellow cloth binding and red lettering looked shabby in comparison to his previous novels, also published by Constable. Although it was not an instant success, it had respectable sales during Stoker's lifetime. It went through eight editions over the next eleven years, including a cheap paperback edition published in 1901.

Initially, *Dracula* received mixed reviews; the *Athenaeum* reported that although Stoker had "a certain degree of imaginative faculty," his novel lacked "constructive art in the higher literary sense. It reads at times like a mere series of grotesquely incredible events." Yet, other readers found the novel delightfully frightening. A reviewer for the *Pall Mall Gazette* wrote: "It is excellent. One of the best things in the supernatural line that we have been lucky enough to hit upon." Sir Arthur Conan Doyle, too, was enthusiastic: "[*Dracula*] is the very best story of *diablerie* which I have read for many years. It is really wonderful how with so much exciting interest over so long a book there is never an anticlimax." Despite the uneven response to *Dracula*, Stoker promoted the book tirelessly, sending more than five hundred presentation copies to his friends and acquaintances.

Over the years, *Dracula* as a work of literature has been fertile ground for scholars and critics. The work has been viewed from every possible critical perspective; twentieth-century readers have examined the novel's treatment of repressed sexuality, homoeroticism, oral fixation, the occult, satanic imagery, gender inversion, Oedipal conflicts, and bisexuality. One modern critic has called *Dracula* "a kind of incestuous, necrophilious, oral-anal-sadistic all-in-all wrestling match." Stoker, who fully supported the censorship of "unclean" books, would be shocked to learn what has been said about his vampire novel. In an 1897 letter to W. E. Gladstone, Stoker explained that there was "nothing base" in *Dracula;* he went on to say that "the book is necessarily full of horrors and terrors but I trust these are calculated to cleanse the mind by pity & terror." Victorian readers, who found nothing objectionable in the work, viewed *Dracula* as an adventure story about the power of good over evil. The controversial layers of meaning that other readers have found beneath the surface of the text remained hidden until well after Stoker's death.

"My dear, it is splendid, a thousand miles beyond anything you have written before, and I feel certain will place you very high in the writers of the day—the story and style being deeply sensational, exciting and interesting.... No book since Mrs. Shelley's 'Frankenstein' or indeed any other at all has come near yours in originality, or terror...."

CHARLOTTE STOKER, *in a letter to her son Bram Stoker, 1897*

Stoker never lived to see the overwhelming, long-term success of his vampire novel. He died of "exhaustion" on 20 April 1912, leaving a modest estate of £4,723 to his widow, Florence. News of his passing was largely overshadowed by the sinking of the *Titanic* six days earlier. Since his death, *Dracula* has never been out of print. The novel has inspired countless stage productions and more than two hundred film adaptations. Few other works of literature have been so warmly embraced by mainstream popular culture. As we celebrate the 100th anniversary of the publication of this horror classic, it seems that the legacy of *Dracula* has just begun.

DRACULA
(London: Archibald Constable and Company, 1897). First edition.

This rare copy of the first edition of *Dracula* is still in its original dust jacket.

DRACULA
(London: Archibald Constable and Company, 1897). First edition. Copy inscribed to Lord Tennyson [Hallam Tennyson, son of the poet].

Stoker presented and inscribed this copy of the first edition of *Dracula* to Hallam Tennyson in July 1897. Stoker, who first met Alfred, Lord Tennyson almost twenty years earlier, was fascinated by the aging poet's long, protruding canine teeth, which reminded him of "vampire's forks."

DRACULA
(New York: Doubleday & McClure Co., 1899). First American edition.
On loan from The Book Sail, Orange, California

Dracula remained unpublished in America until 1899, two years after the novel first appeared in England. This rare copy of the first American edition, signed by Stoker, still has a partial dust jacket.

SELECTED BIBLIOGRAPHY

Belford, Barbara. *Bram Stoker: A Biography of the Author of Dracula.* New York: Knopf, 1996.

Clover, David. *Vampires, Mummies, and Liberals: Bram Stoker and the Politics of Popular Fiction.* Durham: Duke University Press, 1996.

Dalby, Richard. *Bram Stoker: A Bibliography of First Editions.* London: Dracula Press, 1983.

Eddy, Beverley D. (ed.). *Dracula: A Translation of the 1488 Nürnberg Edition.* Philadelphia: The Rosenbach Museum & Library, 1985.

Farson, Daniel. *The Man Who Wrote Dracula: A Biography of Bram Stoker.* London: Michael Joseph, 1975.

Florescu, Radu R. and Raymond T. McNally. *In Search of Dracula.* Greenwich, Conn.: New York Graphic Society, 1972.

Frayling, Christopher. *Vampires: Lord Byron to Count Dracula.* London: Faber and Faber, 1991.

Irving, Laurence. *Henry Irving.* London: Faber and Faber, 1951.

Leatherdale, Clive. *Dracula: The Novel and the Legend.* Wellingborough, Northamptonshire: The Aquarian Press, 1985.

Ludlam, Harry. *A Biography of Dracula: The Life Story of Bram Stoker.* London: Foulsham, 1962.

Roth, Phyllis A. *Bram Stoker.* Boston: Twayne Publishers, 1982.

Skal, David J. *Hollywood Gothic: The Tangled Web of Dracula from Novel to Stage to Screen.* New York: W.W. Norton & Company, 1990.

Wolf, Leonard, ed. *The Essential Dracula.* New York: Penguin, 1993.

Photography	Will Brown
Design	Greer Allen
Typesetting	Highwood Typographic Services
Printing	Hull Printing Company
Binding	Mueller Trade Bindery

This catalog has been printed in a limited edition of 1000 copies.
Of this number 100 are special editions which include
a facsimile reproduction on watercolor paper
of Maurice Sendak's jacket illustration in the exact size
at which it was drawn, numbered and signed by the artist.